Van Gogh's French Journey

Tracing the Footsteps and Encounters

Antonin Paulin-Leclerc

Table of Contents:

Introduction

Vincent van Gogh, a name that echoes through the annals of art history, stands as a testament to the power of creative passion and human resilience. His art, vibrant and emotive, speaks across time and culture, bridging the gap between the past and the present. In this exploration, we embark on a unique voyage through the landscapes of France that played an indelible role in shaping van Gogh's artistic vision.

Van Gogh's journey to France was not just a geographic movement; it was a profound transformation that saw the evolution of his style, palette, and perceptions. The splendor of Paris, the sun-soaked fields of Arles, the contemplative moments in Saint-Rémy, and the bittersweet days in Auvers-sur-Oise — these locales are not mere dots on a map but the very crucibles in which van Gogh's genius simmered and flourished.

As we traverse these paths, we'll encounter not just the scenic vistas that captured van Gogh's brush but also the souls who colored his world. From the vibrant camaraderie shared with Paul Gauguin in the golden fields of Arles to the gentle bond with Dr. Gachet in Auvers-sur-Oise, these encounters speak to the intricate interplay between the artist's life and his art. And let us not forget the ordinary people of Provence whose faces and stories whispered to him in the quietude of each stroke.

Each chapter in this book guides you through a distinct chapter in van Gogh's French odyssey. We shall relive the moments of triumph and turbulence, bask in the luminous hues he painted onto his canvas, and peer into the very heart of his creative fervor. We invite you to walk these paths with us, to feel the winds that rustled through his thoughts, and to catch the echoes of his footsteps as we trace the profound legacy he left upon the landscapes of both art and humanity.

So, dear reader, fasten your imagination's seatbelt and journey with us as we explore "Van Gogh's French Journey: Tracing the Footsteps and Encounters." The paint on his canvases might have dried, but the colors of his story are as vivid as ever, waiting to be uncovered as we journey through the chapters that follow.

Chapter 1: A New Beginning in Paris

Paris: The Allure of the Artistic Haven

In the heart of the 19th-century art world, Paris beckoned to Vincent van Gogh with its promise of inspiration and innovation. The cobblestone streets and grand boulevards of the city would become the canvas upon which his artistic dreams would be painted.

Immersed in Creative Currents

As van Gogh settled into the vibrant rhythm of Paris, he found himself surrounded by a tapestry of artistic diversity. The city's galleries, studios, and cafés hummed with creative energy, offering a rich tapestry of experiences that would shape his artistic path.

Encounters with the Greats

Walking through the halls of Parisian galleries, van Gogh found himself face to face with the works of renowned artists like Monet, Degas, and Pissarro. Each stroke of their brushes resonated with him, igniting a desire to experiment and expand his own artistic vocabulary.

"The Serenity Amidst Activity"

In his letters to his brother Theo, van Gogh expressed the exhilaration he felt amidst the bustling atmosphere of Paris. He wrote, "I feel a certain serenity in the midst of this activity. There's so much here to stimulate thought, and so much that's new." Paris provided the backdrop for his growth, a dynamic environment in which his creativity flourished.

Colors of Transformation

As the city's light played upon its architectural wonders, van Gogh's palette began to shift. The vibrant hues of his earlier works were emboldened by the city's vivid contrasts, marking the beginning of his transition to a more expressive and colorful style.

Paris as a Crucible

Paris was more than just a city to van Gogh; it was a crucible of artistic transformation. The city's influence, a fusion of impressions and experiences, set him on a trajectory toward a new artistic identity. His time in Paris laid the foundation for the remarkable journey that would follow.

In the next chapter, we will venture to the sun-drenched landscapes of Arles, where van Gogh's artistic vision would blossom into a symphony of colors, forever altering the course of his creative voyage.

Chapter 2: A Colorful Sojourn in Arles

Arles: Where Colors Dance in the Southern Sun

Nestled in the embrace of the sun-drenched landscapes of the south of France, Arles welcomed Vincent van Gogh with open arms. It was a place where the vibrant hues of his imagination would find their truest expression.

Sunlit Canvases and Southern Palette

Arles' unyielding sunlight became both a challenge and an inspiration for van Gogh. The intensity of the southern light transformed his palette, breathing life into his canvases with hues that seemed to shimmer and dance. The play of light and shadow across the Provençal fields would forever alter the trajectory of his art.

Chasing Shadows, Capturing Light

Van Gogh's brushstrokes in Arles transcended mere representation; they became a visual symphony of his emotional experience. The bold application of color, often in thick impasto, allowed him to capture the essence of the scene rather than its strict realism. His canvases vibrated with energy, as if the very pulse of the land coursed through his veins.

A Meeting of Minds: Vincent and Paul

In the heart of Arles, van Gogh found not only artistic inspiration but also a kindred spirit in Paul Gauguin. Their friendship and artistic collaboration were both a testament to their shared passion for pushing the boundaries of traditional art. Together, they ignited sparks of creativity, each influencing the other's work in ways that would leave an indelible mark on art history.

Confluence of Styles

Van Gogh's and Gauguin's artistic styles, though distinct, merged in their mutual exploration of color and form. Their creative dialogue produced a series of works that showcased the dynamic interplay between their visions. The vibrant "The Yellow House," a symbolic representation of their artistic camaraderie, stands as a testament to the possibilities that arise when two great minds converge.

The Bittersweet Farewell

Arles, as much as it breathed life into van Gogh's work, also became the stage for his struggles. The famed incident of the severed ear highlighted the emotional turmoil that simmered beneath his vibrant canvases. The intensity of his emotions was as palpable as the colors on his palette.

As we bid farewell to Arles, we leave behind a chapter of profound artistic exploration. The southern landscapes and the friendship with Gauguin became the canvas upon which van Gogh etched his emotions, revealing a raw and uninhibited perspective that would forever alter the course of his journey. In the following chapter, we will delve into the lives and stories of the people of Provence, who became not just subjects on canvas but voices that echoed through his art.

Chapter 3: The People of Provence

Faces of Provence: Portraits Beyond the Canvas

In the sun-kissed realm of Arles, Vincent van Gogh's art found a new dimension as he turned his gaze towards the people who inhabited this charming corner of the world. The locals, once strangers, became not only subjects of his paintings but also the embodiments of the stories and emotions that breathed life into his brushstrokes.

Capturing the Essence: Brushstrokes of Identity

Van Gogh's portraits of the people of Provence were not mere visual representations; they were windows into their souls. Each brushstroke revealed an intricate narrative, a unique blend of the sitter's life and his own interpretation. From weathered hands to pensive expressions, his canvases became mirrors reflecting the essence of the individuals he encountered.

Shared Moments, Shared Lives

In the cafés and marketplaces, van Gogh engaged with the locals, sharing stories and forming connections that transcended the canvas. Madame Ginoux, a figure who graced his portraits, became a symbol of steadfastness and warmth. The café terrace and its patrons found life not just in the paint but also in the laughter and camaraderie shared over conversations.

The Postman and the Night Café

The postman Joseph Roulin, whose portrait series remains an epitome of empathy and humanity, stood as a testament to the profound connections van Gogh forged with those around him. His painting of the Night Café, pulsating with vivid colors and enigmatic energy, encapsulated the atmosphere of the place and its patrons.

Whispers of the Past

Van Gogh's encounters with the people of Provence were not just fleeting moments; they were fragments of lives he internalized. His portraits were more than just artistic endeavors; they were conversations with history, echoes of shared stories, and an exploration of the human experience.

As we explore the lives and stories of the people who left an indelible mark on van Gogh's journey, we enter a realm where art and humanity intertwine. Each portrait becomes a chapter of its own, a visual ode to the individuals who colored his world with their presence. In the upcoming chapter, we will delve into the turbulence and triumphs of van Gogh's time at Saint-Rémy-de-Provence, where his art continued to flourish even amid personal challenges.

Chapter 4: Turbulence and Triumphs in Saint-Rémy

Amidst the Asylum: A Canvas of Struggles and Resilience

In the tranquil landscapes of Saint-Rémy-de-Provence, Vincent van Gogh's life took a poignant turn as he confronted both personal demons and a world of artistic possibilities. Confined within the walls of an asylum, his spirit soared even as his mind grappled with turmoil.

The Artist's Sanctuary

The asylum in Saint-Rémy provided van Gogh with both shelter and confinement. While grappling with the complexities of his mental health, he sought solace in the natural beauty that surrounded him. The ethereal olive groves, the restless skies, and the enchanting garden of the institution became his new muse.

Brushstrokes of Inner Turmoil

Van Gogh's time in Saint-Rémy was marked by an intense internal struggle, mirrored in his art. His swirling brushstrokes and vivid colors captured not only the external world but also his inner emotional landscape. Each canvas was an unfiltered expression of his state of mind, a testament to the depth of his creativity.

Art as a Beacon of Light

Despite his challenges, van Gogh's artistic spirit remained undaunted. Art became his lifeline, a means to process his emotions and channel his energies. His iconic works from this period, such as "Starry Night" and "Irises," are a testament to his unwavering commitment to his craft, even when faced with adversity.

The Healing Power of Creation

Creating art became a form of therapy for van Gogh, an avenue through which he found moments of calm amidst the storm. His paintings were not just an outlet for his pain; they were also a beacon of hope, a testament to his ability to find beauty even in the midst of chaos.

In the next chapter, we'll journey to Auvers-sur-Oise, where van Gogh's final chapter unfolds. It's a poignant exploration of his relationship with Dr. Gachet, the series of portraits he painted, and the complex emotions that define this period of his life.

Chapter 5: Auvers-sur-Oise and the Final Chapter

Auvers-sur-Oise: A Tranquil Retreat and the Shadows Within

In the picturesque village of Auvers-sur-Oise, Vincent van Gogh sought refuge from the storms that had marked his journey. It was a place of respite and reflection, where the serenity of the countryside juxtaposed with the tumult within his soul.

A Portrait of the Doctor: Friend and Muse

Dr. Paul Gachet, a physician with a deep appreciation for art, became both a confidant and a subject for van Gogh. Their relationship was a complex blend of camaraderie and vulnerability, reflected in the series of portraits the artist painted. Through these works, van Gogh's brushstrokes captured not just Gachet's physical presence, but the intricate layers of their connection.

Eternalizing Emotions on Canvas

The portraits of Dr. Gachet stand as a poignant reflection of van Gogh's emotional state during this period. The colors, the contours, and the expressions on Gachet's face became a canvas upon which van Gogh painted his own inner turmoil. These portraits are a testament to the depth of the artist's empathy and the intimacy of their bond.

Whispers of Farewell

Tragically, Auvers-sur-Oise also became the stage for van Gogh's final act. The circumstances surrounding his death remain a subject of speculation and mystery. His departure from this world was as enigmatic as the landscapes he painted, leaving behind a legacy of brilliance tinged with tragedy.

Legacy of a Starry Night

Vincent van Gogh's influence didn't wane with his passing; instead, it grew brighter with time. His art, once considered unconventional, became a touchstone for the modern and contemporary art movements. The vivid colors, the emotive brushwork, and the raw honesty of his work spoke to generations of artists who followed.

In the concluding chapter, we'll reflect on the enduring impact of Vincent van Gogh's journey, both as an artist and as a symbol of the complexities of the human spirit. His story is one of transformation, turbulence, and ultimately, triumph through his art.

Chapter 6: Legacy and Influence

Eternal Echoes: Vincent van Gogh's Lasting Impact

As the final strokes of his artistic journey settled, Vincent van Gogh left behind a legacy that transcends time and borders. His art, once met with indifference, now stands as a testament to the enduring power of creativity and the unyielding spirit of the artist.

Shaping the Canvas of Modern Art

Van Gogh's impact on modern and contemporary art is immeasurable. His innovative use of color and texture, his willingness to push the boundaries of traditional techniques, and his ability to distill emotion onto canvas laid the foundation for artistic movements that followed. His influence on expressionism, fauvism, and beyond is a tribute to the timelessness of his vision.

From Canvas to Consciousness

Beyond the canvas, van Gogh's life story has become a source of inspiration for individuals navigating their own journeys. His struggles with mental health, his dedication to his craft, and his relentless pursuit of his artistic truth resonate with those who seek authenticity and passion in their pursuits.

A Source of Endless Inspiration

Van Gogh's work continues to captivate and inspire artists and art enthusiasts worldwide. Museums and galleries are adorned with his masterpieces, drawing crowds who seek to immerse themselves in the world he created. His sunflowers, starry nights, and evocative landscapes act as portals, transporting viewers to a realm of emotion and imagination.

The Unfinished Symphony

While van Gogh's life was cut short, his art is an ongoing conversation that transcends generations. The brushstrokes he left behind serve as brushstrokes of hope, reminding us that even in moments of darkness, beauty can be found. His legacy is a testament to the power of the human spirit to endure, create, and illuminate.

In the final moments of this journey, we reflect on the colors and emotions that Vincent van Gogh brought to life. His art remains a symphony that echoes through time, inviting us to step into the canvas of his world and find our own connection to the universal language he painted.

Conclusion

The journey we've embarked upon through the life and art of Vincent van Gogh has taken us on a voyage through vibrant landscapes, swirling emotions, and the timeless resonance of creativity. From the streets of Paris to the sun-soaked fields of Arles, from the intimate portraits of Provence to the contemplative moments of Saint-Rémy, and finally, to the bittersweet chapters in Auvers-sur-Oise, van Gogh's story has unfolded in hues both vivid and poignant.

Van Gogh's journey was not just a physical exploration; it was a pilgrimage of the soul. It was a testament to the transformative power of art and its ability to capture the human experience in all its complexity. Through his eyes and brushstrokes, we've witnessed the convergence of personal turmoil and artistic triumph, a narrative that continues to resonate across time and space.

As we close this chapter of exploration, we are reminded that van Gogh's legacy is not confined to the pages of history or the walls of museums. It lives within the boundless capacity of art to transcend language and culture, to evoke emotions and provoke thoughts that ripple through generations. His work invites us to engage in a dialogue not just with the canvas, but with our own perceptions, emotions, and dreams.

Van Gogh's journey is not just his; it's ours as well. As we reflect on the landscapes he painted, the faces he immortalized, and the emotions he articulated, we find fragments of ourselves in his art. His story is an invitation to embark on our own journeys of self-discovery, resilience, and creative expression.

In the footsteps of van Gogh, we embrace the colors of existence—the bright yellows of joy, the deep blues of introspection, and the fiery reds of passion. His art reminds us that even in the darkest of nights, stars still shine. As we bid adieu to this narrative, let us carry forward the legacy of Vincent van Gogh, allowing his art to illuminate our paths and inspire us to paint our own stories on the canvas of life.

Thank you for accompanying us on this journey, and may the colors of van Gogh's art forever illuminate your own artistic odyssey.

Appendix: Chronology of Vincent van Gogh's Life

1853 - 1869: Formative Years

- 1853: Vincent van Gogh is born in Groot-Zundert, Netherlands.
- 1869: Begins his apprenticeship at the art gallery Goupil & Cie.

1873 - 1876: Early Ventures

- 1873: Transfers to London to work at Goupil & Cie.
- 1876: Decides to leave Goupil and briefly teaches in Ramsgate, England.

1880 - 1881: Explorations

- 1880: Moves to Brussels and begins studying art.
- 1881: Settles in Etten for a time, where he starts painting more seriously.

1886 - 1888: Paris and Arles

- 1886: Moves to Paris, discovers Impressionism, and meets influential artists.

- 1888: Moves to Arles in the south of France, where he creates some of his most iconic works.

1889 - 1890: Saint-Rémy-de-Provence

- 1889: Interned at the asylum of Saint-Paul-de-Mausole in Saint-Rémy-de-Provence.
- 1889 - 1890: Creates masterpieces like "Starry Night" and "Irises."

1890: Auvers-sur-Oise

- 1890: Settles in Auvers-sur-Oise, near Paris, under the care of Dr. Gachet.
- Produces numerous paintings, including portraits of Dr. Gachet.

1890: The Final Chapter

- 1890: Vincent van Gogh passes away in Auvers-sur-Oise at the age of 37.

Legacy:

- After his death, van Gogh's work gains recognition and becomes an inspiration for many artists.
- Van Gogh's artistic legacy continues to grow, with his works considered icons of the modern art movement.

This chronology highlights key moments in Vincent van Gogh's life, from his formative years to his residence in iconic places such as Paris, Arles, Saint-Rémy-de-Provence, and Auvers-sur-Oise.